*You know
you're in trouble
when...*

The Wooster Book Company
where minds and imaginations meet

Dedicated to
Paul & Edna Fischer,
my brother Tom,
and all our family

© 2011, 2009 Paul Fischer. All rights reserved.

No part of this book may be used or
reproduced in any manner whatsoever
without prior written permission
of the publisher.

For information address:

The Wooster Book Company
205 West Liberty Street
Wooster, Ohio 44691

Printed in the United States of America
second edition

ISBN: 978-1-59098-730-8

You Know You're in Trouble When...

Baseball

...the umpires get off the bus with the visiting team.

- The home-plate umpire takes his thick glasses off when your team is in the field.

- The umpire calls a balk on your pitcher with no one on base.

- The umpire is wearing the opposing team's warm-up jacket before the game.

- Reruns of your games appear at 3:00 A.M. on COMEDY CENTRAL.

- Your Little League® third baseman beat up the umpire's child yesterday.

- You are catching, and every batter to reach first base steals second.

- The umpire's wife is sitting in the first row with the opposing team manager's wife.

- You call the bullpen for a relief pitcher and a woman answers.

- The home-plate umpire calls the opposing coach "Grandpa."

- In an inter-squad scrimmage, your team loses to the vendors and ushers.

- The umpires offer coaching tips to the opposing team.

- The beer vendor runs out of beer.

- The home-plate umpire overrules the second-base umpire on a close play at second.

- The team mascot is hired as next year's manager.

- The home-plate umpire bumps your catcher as he attempts to throw out a runner stealing second base.

- Two umpires get into a heated argument over where to go for dinner.

- The umpires high-five opposing team players after good plays.

- You attempt to steal second base and there is a runner there.

- The first-base umpire changes his call when the first-base coach yells at him.

- The drug-sniffing dog at the stadium sits and points at your equipment bag.

- The home plate umpire ejects the first base umpire after a call he didn't like.

- The umpire was seen wearing dark glasses and selling pencils in front of the stadium before the game.

- You report off work sick to attend an afternoon game and your picture shows up on the sports page.

- The umpires socialize with the opposing team's dugout between innings.

- As you are signing an autograph for a kid he asks, "Who is he, Mommy?"

- The first-base umpire tells the opposing team's runner when to steal second.

- Your final game of the year is cancelled due to lack of interest.

- The umpire's wife is wearing the opposing team's jersey and hat.

- The cameraman focuses on your dugout while several players are using drugs.

- The home-plate umpire stops a wild pitch by the opposing team when you have the bases loaded.

- The visiting team takes your mascot hostage.

- The home-plate umpire gives the opposing pitcher a ball with a big grease spot.

- Your team is missing from the team standings section of the sports page.

- The umpires were seen having lunch with the opposing team's coaches.

- As a member of the players union, the union files a grievance against you.

- The home plate umpire warms up the opposing team's pitcher before the game.

- The second-base umpire relays your catcher's signals back to the batter.

- You declare free agency and no teams are interested in you.

- Your Little League® pitcher forgot to shave.

- The umpire high-fives the opponent's catcher after a play at the plate.

- You call the bullpen for a relief pitcher and get a recorded message.

- The opposing pitcher refers to the home plate umpire as "Dad."

- Fans request an autograph from the hot dog vendor but none from your team.

- Your pitcher is so wild the home-plate umpire lines up behind the backstop.

- You are having control problems as a pitcher and your stadium organist plays the song, "Hit the Road, Jack."

- The umpire shows up with a six-pack.

- You hit a home run and the fans throw it back.

- The umpire changes his "Out" call when the opponent's player begins to cry.

- The third-base umpire overrules the home-plate umpire on a strike call.

- The umpire puts on his golf shoes in the fifth inning.

- A piece of sandpaper falls out of your pitcher's pocket.

- Your opponent's call for a pitch-out is ruled a strike.

- Your pitching machine has a better curve ball than your pitchers.

- The home-plate umpire points out the location of a pop foul behind the plate to the opponent's catcher.

- You have to pass through a metal detector before entering your dugout.

- The umpire throws batting practice to the opposing team.

- You're playing against Mike's Harley-Davidson® and the umpire shows up on a Harley.

- The umpire tells you this is his fifth game of the day.

- You enter the dugout before the game and there is already a team there.

- You report off work, go to an afternoon game, and receive major publicity for being the one-millionth fan.

- With the bases loaded in the last of the ninth, the batter is 0 for his last 21 at bats, hitting .197.

- The third-base umpire ejects your third-base coach for being too loud.

- The umpires request autographs of opposing team players.

- Television ratings indicate that more viewers watch reruns of "The World's Strongest Man" than your live games.

- Your team average player weight is higher than your team batting average.

- The third-base coach runs through a series of signs for the batter and the umpire warns you for delay of game.

- The opponent's pitcher is the umpire's son.

- You have a no-trade contract and you are traded.

- The home-plate umpire has his right arm in a sling.

- The announcer tells the crowd in the last of the ninth inning that you are working on a no hitter.

- The Jumbotron® shows you missed the crucial call at the plate.

- You learn that you have been traded to another team while watching television.

- The umpires huddle to rule a strike call.

- You have to pay the baseball card company to print your picture.

- Your Little League® player drives to the game.

- Play is stopped for weather and you are winning by two runs, but when play resumes you are losing by two runs.

- The second-base umpire rules your batter's home run a foul ball.

- Your pitcher high-fives the catcher and dislocates his shoulder.

- The umpire calls a time-out when you have the opponent's base runner in a run down.

- The beer vendor keeps walking through your dugout.

- The umpires frisk your team for weapons.

- The umpire changes his call when the fans boo him.

- The TV station switches games during the middle innings for spectator interest.

- The third-base umpire waves the opposing team's runner home on a base hit.

- TV announcers continuously forget the names of your players.

- The umpire hits ground balls to the opponent's infield before the game.

- Your largest crowd shows up for Dime Beer Night.

- The home-plate umpire is wearing an eye patch.

- Your ground crew goes on strike for the same salary as the players.

- Your team bus rear-ends the umpire's car on the way to the game.

- The umpire's wife is your coach's ex-girlfriend.

- Your mascot is wearing the jersey and hat of your opponent.

- The home-plate umpire trips your catcher attempting to catch a pop foul.

- You are playing in a dome and your game is rained out.

- You are umpiring and are wired with a microphone for live action and you get hit in a bad place by a foul ball.

- Your Little League® outfielder was arrested for speeding.

- At the start of each inning the opposing catcher hands the umpire an envelope.

- Your designated hitter is only hitting .103.

- The opposing team takes the field, the home-plate umpire raises a large foam rubber "Number One."

- The umpire calls the game for a rain delay and your team players have to roll out the tarp.

- The opponent's dugout applauds when your relief pitcher reports into the game.

- The home plate umpire failed your history class when he was your student.

- Your offense has hit into six double plays in six innings.

- The umpire arrives with the opponent's manager and takes his golf bag out of the trunk.

- Your designated hitter hits a walk-off home run but misses second base.

- The home-plate umpire rules your runner missed second base.

- No one shows up on Fan Appreciation Day.

- The umpire and the opposing coach are on the same bowling team.

- Your runner tags up at third on a long fly out to center and is thrown out at the plate.

- The umpires are in the congratulations line giving high-fives after a home run made by your opponents.

- The score is tied with one out in the last of the ninth and a runner on third and your center fielder catches a fly ball and throws the ball to his girlfriend in the stands.

- The umpire's wife and the opposing coach's wife are sisters.

- Your team is escorted onto the field at an away game by a SWAT team.

- The umpires at a tough school are all carrying side arms.

- The umpire uses the dugout phone to order a pizza to be picked up in thirty minutes during the second inning.

- The umpire kicks the ball out of your shortstop's glove on a play at second.

- The second-base umpire joins in the infield chatter while your team is batting.

- The third base coach trips your runner rounding third to score.

- The third-base coach runs through a series of signals for the batter, and the batter shakes off the signal.

- The home-plate umpire shows up with a two-beer helmet and straw.

- Your team starts your World Series celebration the night before the game.

- Your batter is called out after a fan catches a foul ball.

- Your pitcher is so wild you have to position an outfielder behind the catcher.

- The umpire warns your third baseman for playing in too close on an obvious bunt situation.

- The opponent's runner scores from first on an infield hit.

- The third-base umpire creates a distraction so the opponent on first base can steal second.

- Your batters have a difficult time hitting the pitching machine's throws.

- The umpire awards home to the opposing team runner after an overthrow to first base.

- Your batter is called out on strikes on an intentional pass.

- Your center fielder calls off the right fielder on a fly ball and fails to make the catch.

- The umpire changes his call when he sees the replay on the Jumbotron®.

- Your best hitter's bat breaks and cork falls out.

- The home-plate umpire uses his chest protector to deflect a throw to the plate.

- Several of your Little League® players are reprimanded for chewing tobacco.

- Your team is not scheduled for national prime time television all season.

- The home-plate umpire is talking on a cell phone while your team is batting.

- The beer vendor is voted as the franchise MVP by the fans.

- The umpire's boss is coaching the opposing team.

- The base umpire tells the opposing team runner when to tag up on a fly ball.

- Your relief pitcher refuses to come into the ballgame.

- You tell the umpire during a heated argument that his breath smells.

- The home-plate umpire signals the opponent's runner to slide at a close play at home plate.

- The opponent's catcher high-fives the umpire after a called third strike.

- You find out kids traded your baseball card for one of Charles Manson.

- The opposing pitcher throws the pitch over the backstop and the umpire calls a strike.

- You walk home the winning run in the bottom of the tenth.

- The umpire gives your leading hitter a sobriety test.

- Your Little League® catcher offers a cigarette to the umpire.

- You intentionally walk an opposing batter and the umpire sends him to third base.

- Your pitching machine is faster than any of your pitchers.

- Your manager is ejected from the game during the pre-game ground rule discussion.

- You call the bullpen for a relief pitcher and you are told, "Wrong number."

- During a late inning in a long ball game, the umpire keeps looking at his watch.

- The umpire interferes with your fielder during a run down.

- The umpire ejects one of your Little League® players for having too much bubble gum in his mouth.

- The third base umpire trips your runner who is rounding third base with the winning run.

- Your batter is hit by a pitch and the umpire calls a strike.

- The umpires appear in your opponent's team picture.

- The opponent's mascot is called on to pinch hit.

- Your Little League® pitcher drops his driver's license at home plate.

- When your seats are next to the guy with the bass drum.

Basketball

... the referee blocks one of your player's shots.

- The scoreboard operator at an away game sounds the buzzer and calls a foul on your team.

- One of the officials takes off his glasses before tip-off.

- None of your family wants complimentary tickets for your tournament game.

- Your opponent forgets to dribble and the official forgets to blow his whistle.

- The referee's daughter is a pom-pom girl for your opponent's dance squad.

- The referee stands on your center's foot during a jump ball.

- One of the officials has his leg in a cast.

- The referee high-fives the opposing team's coach after calling a technical foul on your team.

- None of the officials has a whistle.

- The referee bumps your ball handler out-of-bounds.

- The referee signals a three point award on an opponent's lay-up.

- There is more action in your basketball pre-game warm-up than in the game.

- The referee calls a jump ball while your guard is dribbling down the floor.

- Your team is given a technical foul during player introduction.

- Your best player has four fouls in the first ten minutes.

- You get knocked down while attempting a lay-up and the referee starts a ten-count.

- You find out the referees have a large bet on your opponent.

- Your guard who is driving for a lay-up ends up on his back under the basket and is charged with a foul.

- The scoreboard operator keeps "forgetting" to start the clock in the last two minutes.

- The referee calls time-out when an opposing player is trapped in the back court.

- The referee high-fives your opponent's big man after a slam dunk.

- You recognize the referee as the guy you flipped-off in the parking lot.

- At an away game, the referee is recognized at halftime for his school loyalty.

- The referee requests to have his picture taken with your opponent's high scorer.

- Your college team plays a local high school team in a charity game and loses.

- The referee dives to keep the ball in-bounds for the opposing team.

- During a youth game the referee sits in a chair at mid-court.

- The referee hands scissors to the opposing coach to cut down the nets before the game starts.

- After a controversial foul, your player is charged because the possession arrow favors the opponent.

- Your opponents put their team mascot in the game in the third quarter.

- The referees huddle with the opposing team and draw on the chalk board.

- You have possession of the ball and the referee begins to count down the seconds on the shot clock 5-4-3, when there are actually fifteen seconds left.

- Your coach guarantees a win in the playoff game.

- The referees are intimidated at an away game and don't go past half-court.

- The referee calls a technical foul on two of your players while your team is warming up.

- Your subs refuse to go in the game.

- You find out two of the three officials are the opposing coaches' brothers.

- The referee allows your opponent's basket after time expires.

- You attempt to leave the locker room to go to the court for pre-game warm-up and the door is locked.

- The referees are telling jokes and back-slapping with the opposing coach.

- During an away game spectators walk across the floor while play is going on.

- The opposing team cheerleaders socialize with the referees during non-play.

- One of the referees stands in front of your big man so he can't get the ball.

- Your guard is called for traveling and is charged with a foul.

- The referee stops your three-on-one fast break.

- The referee deflects your team's pass to the opponents.

- The referees warm-up shooting lay-ups with the opposing team.

- One referee is making ninety percent of the calls.

- Your team enters the court and your pep band plays "Na Na Hey Hey Kiss Him Goodbye."

- The referee allows the opponent's big man who has fouled-out to reenter the game.

- The referee is eating a hot dog during the opening tip-off.

- One of the referees sets up as the sixth man of the opponent's zone defense.

- One of your players is called for an over-and-back violation without the ball.

- You find out the referee is the opposing coach's bookie.

- The referee changes his call after a conference with a big guy in the front row.

- The referees at an away game laugh and point at your team while you are warming up.

- The referee refuses to hand your foul shooter the ball.

- During a youth game the referee is talking on his cell phone.

- The referee is recognized as the top contributor to the opponent's school.

- Two opposing players collide, both fall down, and your player is charged with a foul after the referee flips a coin.

- You have more turnovers than points in the first half.

- The opposing team is awarded the ball out-of-bounds after scoring a field goal.

- The referees call time-out and require the opposing team to put in their subs.

- All of the referees at an away game refuse to shake your hand at pre-game.

- The referee has a logo of your opponent's mascot tattooed on his forearm.

- The opposing team is allowed fifteen seconds to advance the ball across the ten-second line.

- One of the referees is sitting with the opponent's cheerleaders rather than watching the game.

- Kids are shooting baskets while action is at the other end of the court.

- A perimeter referee overrules the official under the basket on a call.

- Your guard is knocked out cold while driving for a lay-up but no foul is called.

- Two of three referees play in the opposing team pep band at halftime.

- They tell you the basketball floor has been installed over the ice rink.

- One of your players is called for a three-second violation while playing on defense.

- As a referee, your mob contact advises you that you are not calling enough fouls.

- The referee is at the souvenir stand buying the opponent's products.

- You find out the referee rents his home from the opposing coach.

- Your big man fouls out after his third foul.

Football

... three of the officials march with the opposing team's band at halftime.

- The referee is dating the opposing team's head cheerleader.

- The opposing team's mascot is the referee's son.

- The opposing team's cheerleaders take refreshments to the officials during time-outs.

- The referee repeatedly calls official time-out when the opposing team is out of time-outs in the final two minutes of the game.

- Your offense is penalized on the first play of every possession, resulting in a first down twenty-five yards to go.

- Your pre-game meal is at a fast food restaurant.

- The defensive lineman across from you has on brass knuckles.

- The opposing team's fans hang a noose from the goal post.

- During a time out your quarterback confers with your opponent's coach.

- The opposing coach requests a breathalyzer test for your star running back before the game.

- In the middle of the fourth quarter your team has no first downs.

- The field judge knocks down a pass to your wide-open receiver.

- The officials are wearing orange jumpsuits at an away game.

- You arrive at the stadium and no one is there.

- Your wife and kids are sitting in the opponent's cheering section.

- Your offensive coordinators in the press box are having a pizza party.

- Your cheerleaders throw souvenir shirts and balls into the stands and the fans throw them back.

- Your team pours Gatorade® on the opponent's coach.

- Your offensive coordinator sends in a play to your opponents.

- You win the coin toss and the referee tells you it's the best out of three.

- Your field-goal kicker is injured while celebrating.

- After officiating a game, a crowd is waiting outside the stadium for you.

- The team owner stands beside you on the sidelines.

- The referees bump chests after penalizing your team fifteen yards.

- While going through a rough section of town, your team bus is hit by bullets.

- You see one of the officials give the opposing coach your play book.

- Your mascot has better moves than your running back.

- Your fans chant, "We want the band," at the end of the first quarter.

- Your agent hasn't returned your phone calls for two weeks.

- Your team plane lands at the wrong airport.

- The team doctor is overworked.

- The referee kicks your opponent's fumble out of bounds as you are about to recover it.

- The referee at an away game throws a flag and a wad of money falls out.

- In the middle of the third quarter your offense hasn't crossed midfield.

- You attempt to talk with the quarterback on the sideline phone but he's talking with his girlfriend.

- You're playing against a Catholic school and a rosary falls out of the referee's pocket.

- At an away game, none of your fans show up.

- The referee calls an official time-out as your kicker is ready to kick a last-second field goal.

- The band plays the charge refrain and nobody yells, "Charge!"

- You realize the vitamin health formula you are taking contains steroids.

- The referee gets out of a car that has your opponent's decals on the windows.

- Your team is penalized for excessive celebration after making a first down.

- The opposing team arrives in handcuffs and leg irons.

- Your running back spikes the ball and hits the referee.

- A member of the chain officials trips the running back.

- Your tailgate fans boo your team as you arrive at the stadium.

- You see your coaching position advertised in the local newspaper.

- Your team's first four draft picks play your position.

- Touchdown Jesus puts his thumbs down.

- The opposing team lines up fifteen men on defense for the tenth time.

- During the pre-game fly-over the parachutist with the ball misses the stadium.

- The officials predict in a newspaper article that a record number of flags may be thrown.

- During a measurement for the opponent's first down, you see the chains stretch.

- At an away game, instead of an ambulance, a hearse is present.

- The opposing team's field goal attempt is ten yards short and both officials signal "good."

- Your fans begin to file out after the kick-off.

- The opponent's running back has more yards than your entire offense.

- You are giving your team a motivational talk and they are playing cards.

- Every team wants to schedule you for their homecoming.

- No sportswriters show up for your post-game interview.

- The referee asks you at the beginning of the second half if you want to continue.

- You have to pay for your pre-game meal out of your pocket.

- Your school band plays your opponent's fight song at a pep rally.

- Your booster club members sit in the opponent's section wearing <u>their</u> sports gear.

- One of the officials follows a long gain by your running back with his penalty flag in his hand.

- Your coach asks you when you are planning to retire.

- You are called for a holding penalty on a touchdown run from the one-yard line.

- Your punter kicks the ball into a strong wind and ends up with minus yardage.

- You take a job coaching football at a school whose mascot is a ballerina.

- The visiting team receives a better ovation than your team.

- Your team security officer is scalping tickets.

- The referee taunts your kicker after missing a field goal.

- Your seat at the football game is in front of the guy with the air horn.

- Your fans throw debris at you when you enter the field.

- The PA announcer tells you that your car must be moved immediately or it will be towed.

- Your pass is intercepted and returned for a touchdown by the Burger King® mascot.

- You are a receiver in arena football and the ball and the wall arrive at the same time.

- The cheerleaders spend more time in the weight room than your team does.

- At an away game the bus driver warms up the bus at halftime.

- Your team wins the coin toss, but the referee gives the other team the options.

- Your equipment bus goes to the wrong city for an away game.

- The referee dots the "I" at halftime.

- You're getting beat so bad that the referee instructs the scoreboard operator not to stop the clock.

- Your three buses pull into the hotel to check in and they have never heard of you.

- On a punt, the officials put a half-deflated ball in play.

- The referee has the flag out of his pocket before the game begins.

- Your band leaves the stadium before halftime.

- You are penalized for offsides during pre-game warm-ups.

- Your conversation with your quarterback on the sideline phone is being heard over the PA system.

- The referees sing the opponents alma mater during pre-game ceremonies.

- As coach, your fans put a "for sale" sign and a moving van in your front yard.

- You run through a gaping hole in the line and see a 230-pound linebacker coming at you.

- The referees perform a group celebration in the end zone after your opponent scores a touchdown.

- Your cheerleaders lead cheers for the opposing team.

- Your quarterback is on the LATE SHOW the night before the big game.

- You see the referees tailgating with your opponent's fans.

- Your team sportswriter gives your team a better chance of winning the lottery than winning a game.

- During a rain storm the officials provide a dry ball for the opponents but not for you.

- Your tight end has fifty yards in penalties before halftime.

- You kick-off into the end zone and the referees place the ball at the thirty-five-yard line.

- The stadium is three-quarters empty after the band show.

- The referee spikes the ball after your opponent scores a touchdown.

- Your star running back has one-hundred yards rushing sideline to sideline.

- The head linesman laughs every time your team comes to the line of scrimmage.

- The opponent's defense repeatedly hits the running back before he gets the ball.

- Your band is invited to a bowl game but your team isn't.

- The referee and head linesman argue about spotting the ball.

- Your Gatorade® contains alcohol.

- Someone from your bench hits the referee with a snowball.

- Two of your captains are ejected from the game during the coin flip.

- Your band refuses to leave the field at halftime.

- The referees advise you that the replay booth lost tape footage of the disputed play.

- Your team members spend more time in the dining room than in the weight room.

- At an away game, you find cameras and listening devices in your locker room.

- The referees participate in the opposing team's huddles.

- At an away game, four police cruisers and a paddy wagon are in front of your cheering section.

- As coach, the key to your office doesn't work anymore.

- The referee ejects one of your players after a holding call.

- The owner of the team recommends his son to be your offensive coordinator.

- Most of the male members of your band are built better than your linemen.

- Your quarterback changes into his street clothes at half time so he can go to the dance.

- Playing a tough opponent, five ambulances are lined up on your side of the field.

- The back judge sacks your quarterback.

- Your band plays the opposing team's fight song.

- Your bus driver for the away game shows up drunk.

- Your team wins the coin toss, but you are only given the option to kick-off.

- The referees line up for your opponent's autographs during pre-game warm-ups.

- Your coach asks you what your assignment was on the last play.

- The TV announcers have a hard time keeping a straight face when they talk about your team.

- Your offensive coordinator sends a signal to the quarterback and the defense calls out the play.

- Your fans pelt your team with snowballs.

- Your souvenir store has a hard time giving items away.

- The referee signals an opponent's first down after lost yardage on a third down.

- Your offense has negative yardage for the past six games.

- You're getting beat so bad the officials quit calling penalties.

- The game officials predict in a newspaper article that your team will lose by at least three touchdowns.

- Your running back trips over the yard stripe.

- Your receiver spikes the ball before crossing the goal line.

- Your band is in better condition than your football team.

- Your quarterback's agent tells you what plays you can and cannot call.

- You are taken off the field with an injury and the crowd cheers.

- The referees high-five one another after calling a penalty on your team.

- As coach, your likeness is hanged and burned in effigy after a game.

- During a snow storm your defensive line makes a snowman.

- You keep hearing beeping noises on your sideline head set.

- Your band has better moves than your football team.

Hockey

...you notice your team's skates have been switched and they all have double blades.

- The Zamboni® enters the ice rink during the middle of the period.

- The referee stops one of your team's passes along the boards with his skate.

- The opponent's power play is over and your player can't get out of the penalty box.

109

- The opponent's goalie shows up with a skull and crossbones face mask.

- Your team enters the ice and all fall into a pile.

- The referee allows your opponent to throw the puck into the goal.

- The arena has an inch of water over the ice.

- The referee stops your shot into an open net with his skate.

- The referee high-fives your opponent's player who just leveled your goalie.

- During a fight the referee slugs your player.

- Your goalie not only has his water bottle but also a lunch pail on the goal net.

- The referee holds the stick of your player making a shot.

- The opponent's penalty box is supplied with sandwiches and beer.

- The game is so boring, the spectators chant for the Zamboni®.

- One of your players trips the referee with his stick.

- The referee stops action as your team advances on a three-on-one break.

- The referees skate better than your team.

- The referee knocks the net off the posts as you are about to score.

- As the referee skates by your bench, he elbows several of your players.

- Your opponent high-fives the referee when he calls a penalty on your team.

- Your goalie's water bottle contains alcohol.

- During a fight the referee holds your player while the opponent hits him.

- The referee picks up a broken stick on the ice and shoots at your goal.

- You realize your goalie has on roller blades.

- The referee high-fives your opponent after a fight with one of your players.

- The Zamboni® operator gets a better reception than your team.

- The referee checks one of your players into the boards.

- You have a power play and the referee kicks the puck to the other end of the ice.

Golf

... you are finishing
the final hole of the golf
tournament and the gallery
is at another hole.

- You discover that your caddy left your putter on the last hole.

- The golf cart you rented has only a reverse gear.

- You blast out of a sand trap with a wedge and look down and the ball is still there.

- You drop a penalty golf shot over your shoulder and it rolls back into the pond.

- Your caddy gets caught throwing your ball out of the woods.

- You are leading by one stroke and you hear a loud cheer from the gallery on the green behind you.

- You attempt to hit your golf shot around a tree and you hear a thud.

- Your favorite hole is the nineteenth hole.

- You chip onto the green and you are so far from the hole your caddy hands you a driver.

- The divot goes farther than your ball.

- In a golf tournament you get caught stepping on your opponent's ball.

- You are caddying in a tournament and you receive a cell phone call while your player is putting.

- Your 300+ yard drive in the fairway is picked up by the golf ball machine.

- You enter the rough to play a shot and you slide down a five-foot incline.

- The caddies for your foursome are watching TV in the clubhouse bar.

- You hit your golf ball backwards on your backswing.

- You are unable to ride in your golf cart because your caddy and his girlfriend are in it.

- A double bogie is your best hole of the day.

- Your approach shot to the final green hits the club house.

- Your caddy guesses you are about 150–200 yards from the green.

- You hit a golf shot and see the gallery scramble.

- Your caddy shows up with hip waders and mosquito netting.

- You have to push your golf cart after the third hole.

Miscellaneous

... you are fighting an opponent who is escorted into the ring by two police officers.

- As a boxer, your opponent didn't take an agreed upon dive.

- As a boxer, you can't see out of one of your eyes.

- You are boxing and are knocked down and the referee starts the count at six.

- You are boxing and your opponent hits you wherever and whenever he wants to.

- You are the boxing champion and you get knocked out by your sparring partner.

- The referee compliments your opponent's robe.

- Your manager doesn't place your stool in the corner between rounds.

- During the pre-fight instructions, the referee winks at your opponent.

- You knock your boxing opponent down and the referee helps him up.

- The Timer pulls your stool out from under you as you attempt to sit down.

- Your boxing opponent's entrance song is the funeral march.

- The referee tells you during the round that your shoestring is untied.

- You touch gloves with your opponent at the start of the fight and feel a hard object.

- You are boxing and your manager is shouting instructions to your opponent.

- The referee raises your opponent's hand before the judges' decision is announced.

- You are boxing, the referee separates you as you have your opponent in trouble against the ropes.

- The guy you are boxing is nicknamed "Killer."

- You are called for a low blow foul after hitting your opponent in the ribs.

- You hear the referee tell your opponent how far ahead he is on the score card.

- Nobody cheers as you enter the ring.

- You knock your opponent down with two minutes to go in the round and he is saved by the bell.

- As a boxer, your opponent who was supposed to take a dive won.

- During the pre-fight instructions the referee looks right at you as he says, "Protect yourself at all times."

- The referee ends the round early after you stagger your opponent.

- You are boxing, the referee is giving your opponent instructions.

- As a boxer, your manager and cut man aren't in your corner between rounds.

- You are the sparring partner for the champion and he gets highly upset with you.

- The referee calls your knock down of your opponent a slip.

- You hear your boxing manager call 9-1-1.

- Your horse refuses to come out of the starting gate.

- Your sulky finishes ahead of your horse.

- In a photo finish your horse stops and smiles.

- Your horse is in front of the starter gate in a trotting race.

- The jockey on your racehorse is using an electric prod instead of a whip.

- Your racehorse enters the track and has a feed bag on.

- Your horse and sulky are thirty yards behind the starter gate car.

- You realize in the starting gate that your saddle is on backwards.

- Your horse follows the starters gate car off the track.

- Your horse won't come out of its stall.

- Your sulky has a flat tire.

- You attempt to enter your horse into the starting gate and all the positions are taken.

- The drivers of the two lead sulky's are holding hands.

- Your door of the starting gate doesn't open.

- The seat on your sulky falls off.

- The starters gate car suddenly stops.

- You make a pit stop during the yellow flag and your pit crew is out to lunch.

- You enter the pit during a yellow flag in third place and when you leave, you are in twenty-third place.

- The race car in front of you has Student Driver signs on it.

- You make a pit stop in a **NASCAR**® race and your pit crew tells you, you need a tune up.

- You attempt to leave your pit after a pit stop and your pit crew hands you a bill.

- You wreck your stock car on the victory lap.

- You bring your **NASCAR**® racer onto the track and find out the race is for Indy racers.

- You make a pit stop during the yellow flag and two of your pit crew have on a rival's uniform.

- You attempt to leave your pit after a pit stop, but the jack is still under your car.

- You attempt to pull into your pit during a yellow flag but your pit crew is holding up the wrong car number.

- Your **NASCAR**® driver insists his girlfriend rides with him during the race.

- After taking ten minutes to complete a pit stop, your pit crew high-fives a rival pit crew.

- Your pit crew puts on a tire inside out.

- You make a pit stop during a yellow flag and one of your pit crew members begins an oil change.

- You are in the pole position and your car stalls as the starter waves the green flag.

- You attempt to pull into your pit during a yellow flag and there is already a car there.

- The judge at the dog show asks you if your dog can do anything else besides bark.

- Your dog rolls over when you say sit.

- The judge at the dog show looks like your competitor's dog.

- You trip and fall over your leash while showing your dog.

- A cat gets loose in the dog show.

- The judge at the dog show gives your competitor's dog a biscuit.

- Your dog humps the judge's leg.

- It's time to show your dog and you can't get the cage open.

- Your competitor's dog shakes the judge's hand.

- Your lane in the one hundred yard dash has hurdles in it.

- You are running a relay event and you have a baton in each hand.

- You break the shot put world record and the shot bounces three times.

- You realize you're the only runner following the cross country course markings.

- You attempt to hand the baton to the relay anchor runner who is not there.

- You are whitewater rafting and the channel in front of you is narrower than the raft.

- You are kayaking in the ocean and realize you are being followed by a shark.

- The wave you are riding on your surfboard is higher than your house.

- You are backing your boat down the ramp into the lake and you feel water on your feet.

- You spend the majority of the time in your kayak upside down.

- As an ultimate fighter, you are on your back with four minutes left in the round.

- As an ultimate fighter, the last thing you saw was stars.

- In an ultimate fight, the referee is afraid to enter the octagon.

- All the blood on the octagon floor is yours.

- Your opponent in ultimate fighting is wearing a home arrest device.

- In an ultimate fight, the referee releases your submission hold.

- You are an ultimate fighter and you see an ear lying on the floor.

- As an ultimate fighter, you stop all of your opponents punches with your face.

- As an ultimate fighter, the last thing you remember was a kick coming at you.

- You are skiing down a mountain and you see and hear half of the mountain following you.

- Your bobsled driver hands you the steering wheel.

- Your snowboard hits a tree twenty feet off the ground.

- You are riding your luge down the chute and a bobsled is trying to pass you.

- As a rodeo bull-rider, you draw the bull with the 52-0 record.

- You are bull-riding, spectators cheer louder for the bull than they do for you.

- You are running with the bulls in Spain and you feel hot, moist breath on the back of your neck.

- The bullfight crowd cheers for the bull.

- In a tag team wrestling match the referee prevents your partner from reaching your corner.

- You have your wrestling opponent's shoulders on the mat for at least ten seconds and the referee has not called a pin.

- The referee trips you and your opponent is awarded a take down.

- You are wrestling you are identified with a green band and the referees bands are both red.

- After the Ironman swimming event your bicycle is gone.

- You are swimming in the Ironman contest you see a dorsal fin in the water.

- Your bicycle chain breaks during the Ironman contest.

- You are jumping a line of buses on your motorcycle and a crosswind drifts you away from the landing ramp.

- You fall off your bike in a motocross event and see your bike coming right behind you.

- You attempt to jump over twenty buses on your cycle and you miss by one.

- You discover you are bluffing your ace-high poker hand against your opponents three tens.

- You put all of your poker chips into the pot and your opponent high-fives the dealer.

- You are fencing and your opponent is using a real sword.

- Your bowling ball hits the automatic pin spotter.

- The tennis judge asks your opponent if your borderline shot was in or out.

- Your weightlifting competitor moves weights with one hand that you had trouble lifting with two.

- The soccer official gives your cheering section a yellow card.

Acknowledgements

Thanks to my family for putting up with my nonsense,
for their support, and for their input:

Sandy Fischer

Anjie Fischer

Chris Boatner

Troy Boatner

Marianne Fischer

Glenn Galang

Thanks to my grandkids whose participation in sports
helped make this book possible:

Drew Boatner

Amber Boatner
(my entire secretarial staff)

Trent Boatner

Will Horton

Devin Levan

Brianna Galang-Swanson

Thanks to my friends who are too many to name but you know who you are!

Thanks to my coaches who provided me with sports knowledge and insight

Thanks to my teammates who shared winning, losing, hard work, pain, sweat, bruises, laughter, crying, and a lifetime of friendship and love.

Thanks to my teachers who now realize all things are possible.

And thanks to my publisher, David Wiesenberg, who made all this into a book.